Best-L
Depression Era
recipes

Publications International, Ltd.

ISBN-13: 978-1-4508-1276-4
ISBN-10: 1-4508-1276-7

Manufactured in China.

8 7 6 5 4 3 2 1

Preparation/Cooking Times: Preparation times are based on the approximate amount of time required to assemble the recipe before cooking, baking, chilling or serving. These times include preparation steps such as measuring, chopping and mixing. The fact that some preparations and cooking can be done simultaneously is taken into account. Preparation of optional ingredients and serving suggestions is not included.

Contents

Stovetop Suppers

Veggie Beef Skillet Soup

¾ pound ground beef
2 cups coarsely chopped cabbage
1 cup chopped green bell pepper
2 cups water
1 can (about 14 ounces) stewed tomatoes
1 cup frozen mixed vegetables
⅓ cup ketchup
1 tablespoon beef bouillon granules
2 teaspoons Worcestershire sauce
2 teaspoons balsamic vinegar
⅛ teaspoon red pepper flakes
¼ cup chopped fresh parsley

1. Brown beef 6 to 8 minutes in large skillet over medium-high heat, stirring to break up meat. Transfer to plate.

2. Add cabbage and bell pepper to skillet; cook and stir 4 minutes or until cabbage is wilted. Add beef, water, tomatoes, mixed vegetables, ketchup, bouillon, Worcestershire sauce, vinegar and red pepper flakes; bring to a boil. Reduce heat; cover and simmer 20 minutes.

3. Remove from heat; let stand 5 minutes. Stir in parsley before serving. *Makes 4 servings*

Ham and Vegetable Omelet

1 tablespoon butter or margarine, divided
2 ounces (about ½ cup) diced ham
1 small onion, diced
½ medium green bell pepper, diced
½ medium red bell pepper, diced
2 cloves garlic, minced
6 eggs, beaten
⅛ teaspoon black pepper
½ cup (2 ounces) shredded Colby cheese, divided
1 medium tomato, chopped
   Hot pepper sauce (optional)

1. Melt half of butter in 12-inch nonstick skillet over medium-high heat. Add ham, onion, bell peppers and garlic; cook and stir 5 minutes or until vegetables are crisp-tender. Transfer mixture to bowl; set aside.

2. Melt remaining butter over medium-high heat. Pour eggs into skillet; sprinkle with black pepper. Cook about 2 minutes or until bottom is set, lifting edge of egg with spatula to allow uncooked portion to flow underneath. Reduce heat to medium-low. Cover and cook 4 minutes or until top is set.

3. Gently slide omelet onto large serving plate; spoon ham mixture down center. Sprinkle with ¼ cup cheese. Carefully fold 2 sides of omelet over ham mixture. Sprinkle with remaining ¼ cup cheese and tomato. Cut into 4 wedges; serve immediately with hot pepper sauce, if desired.

Makes 4 servings

Macaroni and Cheese Pronto

8 ounces uncooked elbow macaroni
1 can (10¾ ounces) condensed cream of Cheddar cheese
    soup, undiluted
½ cup milk
2 cups diced cooked ham (about ½ pound)
1 cup (4 ounces) shredded Cheddar cheese
½ cup frozen green peas
    Black pepper

1. Cook macaroni according to package directions. Drain and set aside.

2. Meanwhile, combine soup and milk in medium saucepan. Cook and stir over medium heat until smooth.

3. Add ham, cheese, peas and macaroni to soup mixture. Reduce heat to low; cook and stir 5 minutes or until cheese melts and mixture is heated through. Add pepper to taste.   *Makes 4 servings*

Tip: For a special touch, garnish Macaroni and Cheese Pronto with fresh Italian parsley before serving.

Cook's Note: Perfectly cooked pasta should be al dente—tender but still firm to the bite. Test pasta shortly before the time recommended on the package to avoid overcooking.

Prep and Cook Time: 20 minutes

Oxtail Soup with Beer

2½ pounds oxtails
1 large onion, sliced
4 carrots, cut into 1-inch pieces, divided
3 stalks celery, cut into 1-inch pieces, divided
2 sprigs fresh parsley
1 bay leaf
5 peppercorns
4 cups beef broth
8 ounces dark beer
2 cups finely diced baking potatoes
1 teaspoon salt
2 tablespoons chopped fresh parsley (optional)

1. Combine oxtails, onion, half of carrots, one third of celery, parsley, bay leaf and peppercorns in large saucepan. Pour broth and beer over mixture; bring to a boil. Reduce heat to low; simmer, covered, 3 hours or until meat is falling off bones.

2. Remove oxtails and set aside. Strain broth and return to saucepan; skim fat. Add remaining carrots, celery, potatoes and salt; bring to a simmer. Cook 15 to 20 minutes or until vegetables are tender.

3. Remove meat from oxtails and return meat to saucepan; stir until heated through. Sprinkle with chopped parsley.   *Makes 4 servings*

Oxtails are generally veal or beef tails. This inexpensive cut of meat is bony, but very flavorful. Since they're so tough, oxtails require long, slow cooking methods like braising.

Homestyle Skillet Chicken

    1 tablespoon Cajun seasoning
    ½ teaspoon plus ⅛ teaspoon black pepper, divided
    ½ teaspoon salt, divided
    4 chicken thighs
    2 tablespoons vegetable oil
    4 cloves garlic, minced
    8 small red or new potatoes, quartered
   12 pearl onions, peeled*
    1 cup baby carrots
    2 stalks celery, sliced diagonally into ½-inch pieces
    ½ red bell pepper, diced
    2 tablespoons all-purpose flour
    1 cup chicken broth
    ½ cup sherry
    2 tablespoons chopped fresh parsley

To peel pearl onions, drop into boiling water for 30 seconds, then plunge immediately into ice water. The peel should slide off.

1. Combine Cajun seasoning, ½ teaspoon black pepper and ¼ teaspoon salt in small bowl. Rub mixture onto all sides of chicken.

2. Heat oil in large heavy skillet over medium-high heat. Add garlic and chicken; cook until chicken is browned, about 3 minutes per side. Transfer chicken to plate; set aside.

3. Add potatoes, onions, carrots, celery and bell pepper to skillet; cook and stir 3 minutes. Sprinkle flour over vegetables; stir to coat. Slowly add broth and sherry, stirring to scrape up browned bits. Bring mixture to a boil, stirring constantly.

4. Reduce heat to medium-low. Return chicken to skillet. Cover and cook about 30 minutes or until chicken is cooked through (165°F). Increase heat to medium-high; cook 5 minutes or until sauce is thickened. Season with remaining ¼ teaspoon salt and ⅛ teaspoon black pepper. Sprinkle with parsley. *Makes 4 servings*

Retro Beef and Veggie Stew

3 teaspoons olive oil, divided
12 ounces boneless beef top sirloin, cut into bite-size pieces
2 medium carrots, quartered lengthwise and cut into
    2-inch pieces
1 medium green bell pepper, coarsely chopped
6 ounces green beans, cut into 2-inch pieces
1 can (about 14 ounces) Italian-style stewed tomatoes
1 cup beef broth
8 ounces new potatoes, cut into bite-size pieces
3 teaspoons instant coffee granules, divided
2 tablespoons all-purpose flour
¾ teaspoon salt
¼ teaspoon black pepper

1. Heat 1 teaspoon oil in Dutch oven over medium-high heat. Brown beef 6 to 8 minutes, stirring to break up meat. Drain fat. Transfer to plate.

2. Add remaining 2 teaspoons oil, carrots, bell pepper and green beans to Dutch oven; cook and stir 4 minutes or until edges begin to brown. Add tomatoes, broth, potatoes and 1 teaspoon coffee granules; bring to a boil. Reduce heat. Add beef; cover and simmer 20 minutes or until potatoes are tender.

3. Remove from heat; stir in remaining 2 teaspoons coffee granules, flour, salt and black pepper. Cook, uncovered, 10 to 15 minutes or until thickened. *Makes 4 servings*

Smothered Salisbury Steak

2 teaspoons olive oil
1 large sweet onion, thinly sliced
½ teaspoon salt, divided
½ teaspoon ground black pepper, divided
1 pound ground beef
½ cup fresh bread crumbs (1 slice bread)
1 clove garlic, minced
1 egg white
1 tablespoon Worcestershire sauce
½ cup beef gravy, heated

1. Heat oil in large nonstick skillet over medium-high heat. Add onion; cook and stir 3 minutes or until onion is softened. Add ¼ teaspoon salt and ¼ teaspoon pepper; cook and stir 3 minutes over medium heat or until onions are golden brown. Transfer to plate.

2. Combine beef, bread crumbs, garlic, egg white, Worcestershire sauce, remaining ¼ teaspoon salt and ¼ teaspoon pepper. Mix lightly but thoroughly; shape into 4 oval patties about ½-inch thick.

3. Heat same skillet over medium heat; add patties. Cook 6 to 7 minutes per side or until internal temperature reaches 160°F. Transfer to serving plates; top with hot gravy and prepared onions.
Makes 4 servings

Serving Suggestion: Serve with a wedge of iceberg lettuce dressed with thousand-island dressing and warm crusty French rolls.

Chicken Barley Soup

1 teaspoon olive oil
1 package (8 ounces) sliced mushrooms
¾ cup chopped onion
¾ cup chopped carrot
¾ cup chopped celery
2 cloves garlic, minced
4 cups chicken broth
1 cup chopped cooked chicken
½ cup uncooked quick-cooking barley
1 bay leaf
¼ teaspoon black pepper
¼ teaspoon dried thyme
Juice of 1 lemon
Parsley (optional)

1. Heat oil in Dutch oven over medium-high heat. Add mushrooms, onion, carrot, celery and garlic; cook and stir 5 minutes.

2. Stir in broth, chicken, barley, bay leaf, pepper and thyme. Bring to a boil. Reduce heat; cover and simmer 25 minutes or until vegetables are tender.

3. Remove and discard bay leaf. Stir in lemon juice and sprinkle with parsley. *Makes 8 servings*

Pork Schnitzel

4 boneless pork chops, trimmed, cut ¼ inch thick
½ cup cornflake or cracker crumbs
1 egg, lightly beaten
Salt and black pepper
2 to 4 tablespoons olive oil, divided
⅓ cup lemon juice
¼ cup chicken broth

1. Preheat oven to 200°F. Place ovenproof platter or baking sheet in oven. Place pork chops between layers of waxed paper; pound with smooth side of mallet to ⅛-inch thickness.

2. Place crumbs in shallow bowl and egg in another shallow bowl. Dip 1 pork chop at a time into egg, then crumbs. Place breaded pork chops in single layer on plate. Sprinkle with salt and pepper.

3. Heat 1 tablespoon oil in large skillet over medium-high heat. Cook pork chops in batches 2 minutes per side or until golden brown and barely pink in center. Transfer to platter in oven to keep warm.

4. Remove skillet from heat. Add lemon juice and broth, stirring to scrape up browned bits. Bring to a boil, stirring constantly, until liquid is reduced to 3 to 4 tablespoons.

5. Remove platter from oven. Pour sauce over meat.

Makes 4 servings

Prep and Cook Time: 20 minutes

Speedy Salmon Patties

1 can (12 ounces) pink salmon, undrained
¼ cup minced green onions
1 egg, lightly beaten
1 tablespoon chopped fresh dill
1 clove garlic, minced
½ cup all-purpose flour
1½ teaspoons baking powder
1½ cups vegetable oil

1. Drain salmon, reserving 2 tablespoons liquid. Place salmon in medium bowl; remove bones and break apart with fork. Add reserved liquid, green onions, egg, dill and garlic; mix well.

2. Combine flour and baking powder in small bowl; add to salmon mixture. Stir until well blended. Shape mixture into 6 patties.

3. Heat oil in large skillet to 350°F. Add salmon patties; cook 4 minutes or until golden brown on both sides. Drain on paper towels. Serve warm. *Makes 6 patties*

> *Canned salmon is extremely convenient to keep on hand. It's super healthy and versatile. Use in place of canned tuna to make salads, casseroles and pasta dishes.*

13

Chicken Chop Suey

1 package (1 ounce) dried black Chinese mushrooms
3 tablespoons soy sauce
1 tablespoon cornstarch
1 pound boneless skinless chicken breasts or thighs,
    cut into 1-inch pieces
½ cup thinly sliced celery
2 cloves garlic, minced
1 tablespoon peanut or vegetable oil
½ cup sliced water chestnuts
½ cup bamboo shoots
1 cup chicken broth
2 cups hot cooked white rice or chow mein noodles
    Thinly sliced green onions (optional)

1. Place mushrooms in small bowl; cover with warm water. Soak 20 minutes to soften. Drain; squeeze out excess water. Discard stems. Cut caps into quarters.

2. Blend soy sauce with cornstarch in cup until smooth.

3. Toss chicken, celery and garlic in small bowl. Heat wok or large skillet over medium-high heat; add oil. Add chicken mixture; stir-fry 2 minutes. Add water chestnuts and bamboo shoots; stir-fry 1 minute. Add broth and mushrooms; cook and stir 3 minutes or until chicken is cooked through.

4. Stir soy sauce mixture and add to wok; cook and stir 1 to 2 minutes or until sauce boils and thickens. Serve over rice. Garnish with green onions. *Makes 4 servings*

Pork in Creamy Mushroom-Onion Sauce

2 tablespoons olive oil, divided
4 bone-in pork chops (about 1½ pounds)
½ teaspoon black pepper
¼ teaspoon dried rosemary
¼ teaspoon garlic powder
8 ounces sliced mushrooms
1 packet (1 ounce) dry onion soup mix
1 cup water
2 teaspoons Worcestershire sauce
2 teaspoons Dijon mustard
¼ cup half-and-half

1. Heat 1 tablespoon oil in large skillet over medium heat. Sprinkle both sides of pork chops with pepper, rosemary and garlic powder. Cook chops on one side about 3 minutes. Transfer to plate, browned side up.

2. Add remaining 1 tablespoon oil and mushrooms to skillet; cook and stir 2 minutes. Stir in soup mix, water, Worcestershire sauce and mustard until well blended. Top with reserved pork chops. Reduce heat. Cover and simmer 8 minutes or until pork chops are barely pink in center. Transfer pork chops to serving platter. Cover and keep warm.

3. Boil mushroom mixture 1 minute or until slightly thickened and reduced to 1¼ cups. Remove from heat; stir in half-and-half. Spoon over pork chops.   *Makes 4 servings*

Serving Suggestion: Serve with cooked egg noodles tossed with green peas and thin slivers of red bell pepper.

Mushroom & Chicken Skillet

**1 pound boneless skinless chicken breasts, cut into bite-size
   pieces**
1 can (about 14 ounces) chicken broth
¼ cup water
2 cups instant rice
½ teaspoon dried thyme
8 ounces mushrooms, thinly sliced
**1 can (10¾ ounces) condensed cream of celery soup,
   undiluted**

Combine chicken, broth and water in 12-inch nonstick skillet;
cook until mixture comes to full boil. Stir in rice and thyme. Place
mushrooms on top. Cover; remove from heat and let stand 5 minutes.
Add soup; cook and stir over low heat 2 minutes or until heated
through.   *Makes 4 servings*

Serving Suggestion: Serve with mixed greens salad and sliced fresh
strawberries.

Corned Beef Hash

2 large russet potatoes, peeled and cut into ½-inch cubes
½ teaspoon salt
¼ teaspoon black pepper
¼ cup (½ stick) butter or margarine
1 cup chopped onion
½ pound corned beef, finely chopped
1 tablespoon horseradish
4 eggs

1. Place potatoes in large skillet; cover with water. Bring to a boil over high heat. Reduce heat to low; simmer 6 minutes. (Potatoes will be firm.) Remove potatoes from skillet; drain well. Sprinkle with salt and pepper.

2. Melt butter in same skillet over medium heat. Add onion; cook and stir 5 minutes. Stir in corned beef, horseradish and potatoes; mix well. Press mixture with spatula to flatten.

3. Reduce heat to low. Cook 10 to 15 minutes. Turn mixture in large pieces; pat down and cook 10 to 15 minutes or until bottom is well browned.

4. Meanwhile, bring 1 inch water to a simmer in small saucepan. Break 1 egg into shallow dish; carefully slide egg into water. Cook 5 minutes or until whites are opaque. Remove with slotted spoon to plate; cover to keep warm. Repeat with remaining eggs.

5. Top each serving of hash with poached egg. Serve immediately.

Makes 4 servings

Skillet Pork Chops with Maple Apples

1 package (12 ounces) uncooked egg noodles
1 teaspoon dried oregano
1 teaspoon dried thyme
½ teaspoon salt
½ teaspoon ground nutmeg
¼ teaspoon black pepper
4 center cut pork chops, cut ½ inch thick
2 tablespoons butter or margarine, divided
1 red apple, cored and sliced
¼ cup maple syrup
2 tablespoons lemon juice
½ teaspoon ground ginger

1. Prepare noodles according to package directions; drain.

2. Meanwhile, combine oregano, thyme, salt, nutmeg and pepper in small bowl; sprinkle over pork chops.

3. Melt 1 tablespoon butter in large skillet. Add pork chops and cook over medium heat 5 to 7 minutes per side or until pork chops are barely pink in center. Remove from skillet and cover to keep warm.

4. Add remaining 1 tablespoon butter and apple to skillet; cook and stir about 3 minutes or until tender. Stir in syrup, lemon juice, ginger and additional salt and pepper to taste. Cook about 2 minutes or until slightly thickened.

5. Serve pork chops and apple mixture over noodles.

Makes 4 servings

Prep and Cook Time: 26 minutes

18

Vegetable Frittata

4½ teaspoons olive oil, divided
¼ cup chopped onion
6 eggs
1 package (10 ounces) frozen chopped spinach, thawed,
   well drained
¾ cup (3 ounces) shredded Cheddar cheese
½ teaspoon salt
⅛ teaspoon black pepper
   Dash ground red pepper
   Dash ground nutmeg

1. Heat 3 teaspoons olive oil in large nonstick skillet over medium heat. Add onion; cook and stir until tender. Remove onion from skillet with slotted spoon; set aside.

2. Lightly beat eggs in medium bowl. Stir in onion, spinach, cheese, salt, black pepper, red pepper and nutmeg.

3. Heat remaining 1½ teaspoons oil in same skillet. Add egg mixture. Cook 5 minutes or until bottom is lightly browned.

4. Place large plate over frittata; invert onto plate. Slide frittata, uncooked side down, back into skillet.

5. Cook 4 minutes or until set. Cut into wedges to serve.

Makes 4 to 6 servings

19

Depression Dinners

Tuna-Macaroni Casserole

1 cup mayonnaise
1 cup (4 ounces) shredded Swiss cheese
½ cup milk
¼ cup chopped onion
¼ cup chopped red bell pepper
⅛ teaspoon black pepper
2 cans (6 ounces each) tuna, drained and flaked
1 package (about 10 ounces) frozen peas
2 cups shell pasta or elbow macaroni, cooked and drained
½ cup dry bread crumbs
2 tablespoons melted butter
Chopped fresh parsley

1. Preheat oven to 350°F.

2. Stir together mayonnaise, cheese, milk, onion, bell pepper and black pepper in large bowl. Add tuna, peas and macaroni; toss to coat well.

3. Spoon into 2-quart casserole. Mix bread crumbs with butter in small bowl and sprinkle over top. Bake 30 to 40 minutes or until heated through. Top with chopped parsley. *Makes 6 servings*

Chicken and Dumplings Stew

2 cans (about 14 ounces each) chicken broth
1 pound boneless skinless chicken breasts, cut into bite-size
   pieces
1 cup sliced carrots
¾ cup sliced celery
1 medium onion, halved and cut into small wedges
3 small new potatoes, cut into cubes
½ teaspoon dried rosemary
½ teaspoon black pepper
¾ cup plus 3 tablespoons all-purpose flour, divided
⅓ cup water
1 can (about 14 ounces) diced tomatoes, drained
1 teaspoon baking powder
¼ teaspoon onion powder
¼ teaspoon salt
1 to 2 tablespoons finely chopped fresh parsley
1 egg
¼ cup milk
1 tablespoon vegetable oil

1. Bring broth to a boil in Dutch oven; add chicken. Cover and simmer 3 minutes. Add carrots, celery, onion, potatoes, rosemary and pepper. Cover and simmer 10 minutes. Combine 3 tablespoons flour and water in small cup. Reduce heat; stir in tomatoes and flour mixture. Cook and stir until mixture thickens.

2. Combine remaining ¾ cup flour, baking powder, onion powder and salt in medium bowl; blend in parsley. Combine egg, milk and oil in small bowl; stir into flour mixture just until moistened.

3. Return broth mixture to a boil. Drop 8 tablespoons of dumpling batter into broth; cover tightly. Reduce heat; cover and simmer 18 to 20 minutes or until toothpick inserted into centers comes out clean.

Makes 4 servings

Polish Reuben Casserole

2 cans (10¾ ounces each) condensed cream of mushroom
   soup, undiluted
1⅓ cups milk
½ cup chopped onion
1 tablespoon prepared mustard
1 jar (32 ounces) sauerkraut, rinsed and drained
1 package (8 ounces) uncooked medium egg noodles
1½ pounds Polish sausage, cut into ½-inch pieces
2 cups (8 ounces) shredded Swiss cheese
¾ cup whole wheat bread crumbs
2 tablespoons butter, melted

1. Preheat oven to 350°F. Grease 13×9-inch baking dish.

2. Combine soup, milk, onion and mustard in medium bowl; stir well.

3. Spread sauerkraut in prepared dish. Top with noodles. Spoon soup mixture evenly over noodles. Top with sausage, then cheese.

4. Combine bread crumbs and butter in small bowl; sprinkle over top. Cover tightly with foil. Bake about 1 hour or until noodles are tender.   *Makes 8 to 10 servings*

Apple Stuffed Pork Loin Roast

2 cloves garlic, minced
1 teaspoon coarse salt
1 teaspoon dried rosemary
½ teaspoon dried thyme
½ teaspoon black pepper
1 boneless center cut pork loin roast (4 to 5 pounds)
1 tablespoon butter
2 large tart apples, peeled, cored and thinly sliced
   (about 2 cups)
1 medium onion, cut into thin strips (about 1 cup)
2 tablespoons packed brown sugar
1 teaspoon Dijon mustard
1 cup apple cider or apple juice

1. Preheat oven to 325°F. Combine garlic, salt, rosemary, thyme and pepper in small bowl. Cut lengthwise down roast almost to, but not through, bottom. Open like a book. Rub half of garlic mixture onto cut sides of pork.

2. Melt butter in large skillet over medium-high heat. Add apples and onion; cook and stir 5 to 10 minutes or until soft. Stir in brown sugar and mustard. Spread mixture evenly onto one cut side of roast. Close halves; tie roast with kitchen string at 2-inch intervals. Place roast on rack in shallow roasting pan. Rub outside of roast with remaining garlic mixture. Pour apple cider over roast.

3. Roast, uncovered, basting frequently with pan drippings 2 to 2½ hours or until thermometer inserted into thickest part of roast registers 155°F. Remove roast from oven; let stand 15 minutes before slicing. (Internal temperature will continue to rise 5° to 10°F). Carve roast crosswise to serve. *Makes 14 to 16 servings*

Serving Suggestion: Serve with Brussels sprouts, buttered noodles tossed with grated Parmesan and a tomato and cucumber salad.

Slow and Easy Weekend Pot Roast

1 boneless pot roast (3 pounds)
¼ teaspoon salt
1 teaspoon black pepper
4 slices bacon, chopped
1 medium onion, sliced
1 tablespoon olive oil
8 ounces sliced mushrooms
1 medium green bell pepper, coarsely chopped
1½ cups pasta sauce
½ cup dry red wine
1½ tablespoons balsamic vinegar
1 tablespoon Worcestershire sauce

1. Preheat oven to 350°F. Sprinkle both sides of roast with salt and black pepper.

2. Heat Dutch oven over medium-high heat. Add bacon; cook and stir until crisp. Transfer bacon to plate. Add roast to Dutch oven; cook 3 to 4 minutes per side or until well browned. Transfer roast to plate with bacon.

3. Add onion and oil to Dutch oven; cook and stir 4 minutes or until onion is translucent. Stir in mushrooms and bell pepper. Remove from heat. Place roast and bacon on top of mushrooms and onion in Dutch oven.

4. Combine pasta sauce, wine, vinegar and Worcestershire sauce in medium bowl; pour over top of roast. Cover and bake 2½ hours or until roast is very tender.   *Makes 8 servings*

Italian-Style Meat Loaf Patties

2 pounds ground beef
1 cup seasoned dry bread crumbs
1 cup pasta sauce, divided
2 eggs
4 tablespoons Parmesan cheese, divided
2 tablespoons dried minced onion
1 package (12 ounces each) wide noodles
2 tablespoons butter, melted

1. Preheat oven to 375°F. Lightly grease large broiler pan.

2. Combine beef, bread crumbs, ½ cup pasta sauce, eggs, 3 tablespoons cheese and onion; mix well. Shape meat mixture into 8 (1-inch-thick) oblong patties. Place on prepared pan. Brush patties with remaining ½ cup pasta sauce. Bake 20 minutes or until internal temperature reaches 160°F.

3. Meanwhile, cook noodles according to package directions; drain. Toss with butter and remaining 1 tablespoon cheese. Serve patties with noodles. *Makes 8 servings*

Prep Time: 5 minutes
Cook Time: 20 minutes

Baked Fish with Potatoes and Onions

1 pound baking potatoes, thinly sliced
1 large onion, thinly sliced
1 small red or green bell pepper, thinly sliced
   Salt and black pepper
½ teaspoon dried oregano
1 pound lean fish fillets, cut 1 inch thick
¼ cup butter or margarine
¼ cup all-purpose flour
2 cups milk
¾ cup (3 ounces) shredded Cheddar cheese

1. Preheat oven to 375°F. Grease 3-quart casserole.

2. Arrange half of potatoes in prepared casserole. Top with half of onion and half of bell pepper. Season with salt and black pepper. Sprinkle with half of oregano. Arrange fish in one layer over vegetables. Arrange remaining potatoes, onion and bell pepper over fish. Sprinkle with salt, black pepper and remaining oregano.

3. Melt butter in medium saucepan over medium heat. Add flour; cook and stir until bubbly. Gradually stir in milk. Cook and stir until thickened. Pour white sauce over casserole. Cover and bake 40 minutes or until potatoes are tender. Sprinkle with cheese. Bake, uncovered, about 5 minutes or until cheese is melted.

Makes 4 servings

Roast Leg of Lamb

3 tablespoons coarse grain mustard
2 cloves garlic, minced*
1½ teaspoons dried rosemary
½ teaspoon black pepper
1 leg of lamb, well trimmed, boned, rolled and tied
   (about 4 pounds)
Mint jelly (optional)

*For a more intense garlic flavor inside the meat, cut garlic into slivers. Cut small pockets at random intervals throughout roast with tip of sharp knife; insert garlic slivers.

1. Line shallow roasting pan with foil. Combine mustard, garlic, rosemary and pepper. Rub mustard mixture over lamb. Place roast on rack in prepared roasting pan.** Preheat oven to 400°F. Roast 15 minutes. *Reduce oven temperature to 325°F; roast about 20 minutes per pound for medium or until internal temperature reaches 145°F.*

2. Transfer roast to cutting board; cover with foil. Let stand 10 to 15 minutes before carving. (Internal temperature will continue to rise 5° to 10°F).

3. Cut strings from roast; discard. Carve into 20 slices. Serve with mint jelly, if desired.   *Makes 10 servings*

**At this point the lamb may be covered and refrigerated up to 24 hours before roasting.

Ask your butcher to prepare the leg of lamb for you. If you call ahead of time, generally a butcher will remove the bone, roll and tie the lamb at no extra charge.

Old-Fashioned Cabbage Rolls

8 ounces ground beef
8 ounces ground veal
8 ounces ground pork
1 small onion, chopped
2 eggs, lightly beaten
½ cup dry bread crumbs
1 teaspoon salt
1 teaspoon molasses
¼ teaspoon ground ginger
¼ teaspoon ground nutmeg
¼ teaspoon ground allspice
1 large head cabbage, separated into leaves
3 cups water
¼ cup (½ stick) butter
½ cup milk, plus additional if necessary
1 tablespoon cornstarch

1. Combine beef, veal, pork and onion in large bowl. Add eggs, bread crumbs, salt, molasses, ginger, nutmeg and allspice; mix well. Add to meat mixture; stir until well blended.

2. Boil water in large saucepan; add cabbage leaves. Boil 3 minutes. Remove with slotted spoon; reserve ½ cup of boiling liquid.

3. Preheat oven to 375°F. Place about 2 tablespoons meat mixture about 1 inch from stem end of each cabbage leaf. Fold sides in and roll up, fastening with toothpicks, if necessary.

4. Heat butter in large ovenproof skillet over medium-high heat. Brown cabbage rolls, 3 or 4 at a time, on all sides. Arrange rolls, seam side down, in single layer in casserole. Combine reserved boiling liquid with butter remaining in skillet; pour over cabbage rolls.

* * * * * * * * * * * * * * * * *

5. Bake 1 hour. Carefully drain accumulated juices from skillet into measuring cup. Add enough milk to equal 1 cup. Pour milk mixture into small saucepan. Stir in cornstarch; bring to a boil, stirring constantly until sauce is thickened. Pour over cabbage rolls.

6. Bake 15 minutes or until cabbage rolls are tender and sauce is bubbly. *Makes 8 servings*

Apple, Bean and Ham Casserole

3 cans (about 15 ounces each) Great Northern beans, rinsed and drained
1 pound boneless ham, cut into 1-inch cubes
1 medium Granny Smith apple, diced
1 small onion, diced
3 tablespoons packed brown sugar
3 tablespoons dark molasses
1 tablespoon Dijon mustard
1 teaspoon ground allspice
¼ cup thinly sliced green onions *or* 1 tablespoon chopped fresh parsley

1. Preheat oven to 350°F. Combine beans, ham, apple, onion, brown sugar, molasses, mustard and allspice in 3-quart casserole; mix well.

2. Cover and bake 45 minutes or until most liquid is absorbed. Sprinkle with green onions before serving. *Makes 6 servings*

Note: This casserole can be covered and refrigerated up to 2 days. To reheat, stir ⅓ cup water into dish. Microwave on HIGH 10 minutes or in preheated 350°F oven 40 minutes until hot and bubbly.

29

* * * * * * * * * * * * * * * * *

Salmon & Noodle Casserole

6 ounces uncooked egg noodles
1 teaspoon vegetable oil
1 medium onion, finely chopped
¾ cup thinly sliced carrot
¾ cup thinly sliced celery
1 can (about 15 ounces) salmon, drained, skin and bones
   discarded
1 can (10¾ ounces) condensed cream of celery soup,
   undiluted
1 cup (4 ounces) shredded Cheddar cheese
¾ cup frozen peas
½ cup sour cream
¼ cup milk
⅛ teaspoon dried dill weed
   Black pepper

1. Preheat oven to 350°F. Cook noodles in large saucepan according to package directions; drain and return to saucepan.

2. Meanwhile, heat oil in large skillet over medium heat. Add onion, carrot and celery; cook and stir 4 to 5 minutes or until vegetables are crisp-tender.

3. Add salmon, onion mixture, soup, cheese, peas, sour cream, milk, dill and pepper to noodles; stir gently until blended. Pour into 2-quart casserole dish. Cover and bake 25 to 30 minutes or until hot and bubbly. *Makes 4 to 5 servings*

Hot Three-Bean Casserole

2 tablespoons olive oil
1 cup coarsely chopped onion
1 cup chopped celery
2 cloves garlic, minced
1 can (about 15 ounces) chickpeas, rinsed and drained
1 can (about 15 ounces) kidney beans, rinsed and drained
1 cup coarsely chopped tomato
1 cup water
1 can (about 8 ounces) tomato sauce
1 to 2 jalapeño peppers,* minced
1 tablespoon chili powder
2 teaspoons sugar
1½ teaspoons ground cumin
1 teaspoon salt
1 teaspoon dried oregano
¼ teaspoon black pepper
2½ cups (10 ounces) frozen cut green beans
Fresh oregano (optional)

*Jalapeño peppers can sting and irritate the skin, so wear rubber gloves when handling peppers and do not touch your eyes.

1. Heat oil in large skillet over medium heat. Add onion, celery and garlic; cook and stir 5 minutes or until tender.

2. Add chickpeas, kidney beans, tomato, water, tomato sauce, jalapeño, chili powder, sugar, cumin, salt, dried oregano and black pepper. Bring to a boil. Reduce heat to low; simmer 20 minutes. Stir in green beans; simmer 10 minutes or until tender. Garnish with fresh oregano. *Makes 12 servings*

Hungarian Beef Stew

¼ **cup vegetable oil**
1 **medium onion, chopped**
1 **cup sliced mushrooms**
2 **teaspoons paprika**
2 **pounds beef top sirloin steaks, ½-inch thick, cut into**
    ½-inch pieces
½ **cup beef broth**
½ **teaspoon caraway seeds**
    Salt and black pepper to taste
1 **cup sour cream**
2 **tablespoons all-purpose flour**
    Hot buttered noodles
    Chopped fresh parsley (optional)

1. Heat oil in 5-quart Dutch oven over medium-high heat. Add onion and mushrooms; cook and stir until onion is soft. Stir in paprika. Remove with slotted spoon; set aside.

2. Brown half of beef in Dutch oven over medium-high heat. Remove with slotted spoon; set aside. Brown remaining beef. Drain fat. Return beef, onion and mushrooms to Dutch oven. Stir in broth, caraway seeds, salt and pepper. Bring to a boil over high heat. Reduce heat to low. Cover; simmer 45 minutes or until beef is fork-tender.

3. Whisk sour cream and flour in small bowl. Whisk sour cream mixture into stew; stir until slightly thickened. *Do not boil.* Serve over noodles. Garnish with parsley.   *Makes 6 to 8 servings*

Bacon and Cheese Rarebit

1½ tablespoons butter
½ cup beer (not dark)
2 teaspoons Worcestershire sauce
2 teaspoons Dijon mustard
⅛ teaspoon ground red pepper
2 cups (8 ounces) shredded American cheese
1½ cups (6 ounces) shredded sharp Cheddar cheese
1 small loaf (8 ounces) egg bread or challah, cut into
    6 (1-inch-thick) slices
12 large slices tomato
12 slices bacon, crisp-cooked

1. Preheat broiler. Line baking sheet with foil.

2. Melt butter in double boiler set over simmering water. Stir in beer, Worcestershire sauce, mustard and red pepper; heat through. Gradually add cheeses, stirring constantly, about 1 minute or until cheeses are melted. Remove from heat; cover and keep warm.

3. Broil bread slices until golden brown. Arrange on prepared baking sheet. Top each serving with tomato and bacon. Spoon about ¼ cup cheese sauce evenly over top. Broil 4 to 5 inches from heat 2 to 3 minutes or until cheese sauce begins to brown. Transfer to individual serving plates. Serve immediately. *Makes 6 servings*

Sides & Breads

Apricot-Glazed Beets

1 pound fresh beets
1 cup apricot nectar
1 tablespoon cornstarch
2 tablespoons cider vinegar or red wine vinegar
8 dried apricot halves, cut into strips
¼ teaspoon salt
    Additional apricot halves (optional)

1. Cut tops off beets, leaving at least 1 inch of stems (do not trim root ends). Scrub beets under running water with soft vegetable brush, being careful not to break skins. Place beets in medium saucepan; cover with water. Bring to a boil over high heat; reduce heat. Cover and simmer about 20 minutes or until just barely firm when pierced with fork. Drain; cool. Rinse pan.

2. Combine apricot nectar and cornstarch in same saucepan. Add vinegar; stir until smooth. Add apricots and salt; cook and stir over medium heat until mixture thickens.

3. Cut roots and stems from beets. Peel, halve and cut beets into ¼-inch-thick slices. Add beet slices to apricot mixture; toss gently to coat. Transfer to warm serving dish. Garnish with additional apricot halves. *Makes 4 servings*

Note: Cut beets on a dinner plate or paper plates instead of a cutting board; the juice will stain the board.

Pull-Apart Rye Rolls

¾ **cup water**
2 **tablespoons butter or margarine, softened**
2 **tablespoons molasses**
2¼ **cups all-purpose flour, plus more for dusting, divided**
½ **cup rye flour**
⅓ **cup nonfat dry milk powder**
1 **package (¼ ounce) active dry yeast**
1½ **teaspoons salt**
1½ **teaspoons caraway seeds**
  Melted butter or vegetable oil

1. Heat water, 2 tablespoons butter and molasses in small saucepan over low heat until temperature reaches 120° to 130°F. Combine 1¼ cups all-purpose flour, rye flour, milk powder, yeast, salt and caraway seeds in large bowl. Stir heated water mixture into flour mixture with wooden spoon to form soft but sticky dough. Gradually add more all-purpose flour until rough dough forms.

2. Turn out dough onto lightly floured surface. Knead 5 to 8 minutes or until smooth and elastic, gradually adding remaining flour to prevent sticking, if necessary. Cover with inverted bowl. Let rise 35 to 40 minutes or until dough has increased in bulk by one third. Punch down dough; divide in half. Roll each half into 12-inch log. Using sharp knife, cut each log evenly into 12 pieces; shape into tight balls. Arrange in greased 9-inch cake pan. Brush tops with melted butter. Loosely cover with lightly greased sheet of plastic wrap. Let rise in warm place (85°F) 45 minutes or until doubled in bulk.

3. Preheat oven to 375°F. Uncover rolls; bake 15 to 20 minutes or until golden brown. Cool in pan on wire rack 5 minutes. Remove rolls to rack; cool.

Makes 24 rolls

* * * * * * * * * * * * * * * * *

Ham Seasoned Peas

1 teaspoon olive oil
½ cup cooked ham, chopped
¼ cup chopped onion
2 cups (about 9 ounces) frozen peas
¼ cup chicken broth
⅛ to ¼ teaspoon dried oregano
⅛ teaspoon black pepper (optional)

1. Heat oil in medium saucepan over medium heat. Add ham and onion; cook and stir 2 minutes or until onion is tender.

2. Stir in peas, broth, oregano and pepper, if desired. Bring to a boil. Reduce heat to low; cover and simmer 4 minutes or until peas are tender. *Makes 4 servings*

Prep Time: 5 minutes
Cook Time: 10 minutes

Cranberry Crunch Gelatin

2 cups boiling water
2 packages (4 serving size each) cherry gelatin
1 can (16 ounces) whole berry cranberry sauce
1½ cups mini marshmallows
1 cup coarsely chopped walnuts

1. Combine boiling water into gelatin in large bowl; stir 2 minutes or until completely dissolved. Chill about 2 hours or until slightly set.

2. Fold cranberry sauce, marshmallows and walnuts into gelatin mixture. Pour into 6-cup gelatin mold. Cover and refrigerate at least 4 hours or until set. Invert onto serving dish. *Makes 8 servings*

* * * * * * * * * * * * * * * * *

* * * * * * * * * * * * * * * * *

Dill Sour Cream Scones

2 cups all-purpose flour
2 teaspoons baking powder
½ teaspoon baking soda
½ teaspoon salt
¼ cup (½ stick) cold butter, cut into small pieces
2 eggs
½ cup sour cream
1 tablespoon chopped fresh dill *or* **1 teaspoon dried dill weed**

1. Preheat oven to 425°F.

2. Combine flour, baking powder, baking soda and salt. Cut in butter with pastry blender or two knives until mixture resembles coarse crumbs. Beat eggs with fork in small bowl. Add sour cream and dill; beat until well blended. Stir into flour mixture until mixture forms soft dough that pulls away from side of bowl.

3. Turn out dough onto well floured surface. Knead 10 times.* Roll dough into 9×6-inch rectangle with lightly floured rolling pin. Cut dough into 6 (3-inch) squares. Cut each square diagonally in half, making 12 triangles. Place triangles 2 inches apart on ungreased baking sheets.

4. Bake 10 to 12 minutes or until golden brown. Cool on wire rack 10 minutes. Serve warm or cool completely.   *Makes 12 scones*

*To knead dough, fold dough in half toward you and press dough away from you with heels of hands. Give dough a quarter turn and continue folding, pushing and turning.

* * * * * * * * * * * * * * * * *

* * * * * * * * * * * * * * * * * *

Dried Fruit Compote

1 cup water
1 cup apple juice
½ cup Rhine wine or additional apple juice
¼ cup packed light brown sugar
2 cinnamon sticks
4 whole allspice berries
4 whole cloves
4 whole black peppercorns
1 package (8 ounces) dried mixed fruit

1. Combine water, apple juice, wine and brown sugar in medium saucepan.

2. Wrap cinnamon sticks, allspice berries, cloves and peppercorns in 8-inch square of double thickness cheesecloth. Tie securely with string; add to saucepan. Stir in dried fruit.

3. Bring to a boil over high heat. Reduce heat to low; cover and simmer 12 to 15 minutes or until fruit is tender, stirring once. Cool; discard cheesecloth bag.

4. Serve compote warm, at room temperature or chilled in small bowls. *Makes 6 servings*

Note: This recipe can be prepared with ground spices instead of whole spices. Substitute ½ teaspoon ground cinnamon for cinnamon sticks, ¼ teaspoon ground allspice for allspice berries, ⅛ teaspoon ground cloves for whole cloves and ⅛ teaspoon freshly ground black pepper for peppercorns. Proceed as directed. Wrap in cheesecloth or add directly to liquid.

* * * * * * * * * * * * * * * * * *

Potato-Carrot Pancakes

1 pound baking potatoes, peeled and shredded
1 medium carrot, shredded
2 tablespoons minced green onion
1 tablespoon all-purpose flour
1 egg, beaten
½ teaspoon salt
⅛ teaspoon black pepper
2 tablespoons vegetable oil

1. Wrap shredded potatoes and carrot in several thicknesses of paper towels; squeeze to remove excess moisture. Combine potatoes, carrot, onion, flour, egg, salt and pepper in medium bowl; mix well.

2. Heat oil in large skillet over medium heat. Drop spoonfuls of potato mixture into skillet; flatten to form thin pancakes. Cook 5 minutes or until browned on bottom; turn and cook 5 minutes or until tender. *Makes about 12 pancakes*

Be careful not to crowd the pan when making these pancakes. Fry in batches to make sure that each pancake has room to get crispy rather than soggy. Use additional oil if needed for the second batch.

Candied Sweet Potatoes

2 medium sweet potatoes (about 2 pounds total), peeled
   and quartered
1 can (8 ounces) crushed pineapple in juice, undrained
½ cup fresh orange juice
¼ cup plus 2 tablespoons packed light brown sugar, divided
2 tablespoons butter, divided
1 tablespoon cornstarch
¼ cup all-purpose flour
¼ cup chopped pecans
¼ teaspoon ground cinnamon

1. Grease 1½-quart shallow baking dish.

2. Place sweet potatoes in large saucepan. Add water to cover. Bring
to a boil over high heat; boil 25 to 30 minutes or until tender. Drain
sweet potatoes; cool 5 minutes. Cut into ¼-inch-thick slices. Place in
prepared baking dish.

3. Meanwhile, combine pineapple, orange juice, ¼ cup brown sugar,
1 tablespoon butter and cornstarch in small saucepan. Cook and
stir over medium heat 6 to 8 minutes or until mixture comes to a
boil and thickens. Reduce heat and simmer for 5 minutes, stirring
occasionally.

4. Preheat the oven to 350°F.

5. Combine flour, pecans, remaining 2 tablespoons brown sugar,
remaining 1 tablespoon butter and cinnamon in small bowl. Spoon
pineapple mixture over sweet potatoes. Sprinkle with nut topping.
Bake 30 to 35 minutes or until heated through.   *Makes 6 servings*

Angel Biscuits

⅓ cup warm water (110°F)
1 package (¼ ounce) active dry yeast
5 cups all-purpose flour
3 tablespoons sugar
1 tablespoon baking powder
1 teaspoon baking soda
1 teaspoon salt
1 cup shortening
2 cups buttermilk

1. Preheat oven to 450°F. Pour water into small bowl. Sprinkle yeast over water and stir until dissolved. Let stand 10 minutes or until small bubbles form.

2. Combine flour, sugar, baking powder, baking soda and salt in large bowl. Cut in shortening with pastry blender or two knives until mixture resembles fine crumbs. Make well in center. Pour in yeast mixture and buttermilk; stir with fork until mixture forms dough.

3. Turn dough out onto lightly floured board. Knead 30 seconds or until dough feels light and soft but not sticky. Roll out desired amount of dough to ½-inch thickness. Cut biscuit rounds with 2-inch cutter. Place biscuits close together (for soft sides) or ½ inch apart (for crispy sides) on ungreased baking sheet. Bake 15 to 18 minutes or until tops are lightly browned. *Makes about 5 dozen biscuits*

Note: If you don't want to bake all the biscuits at once, place biscuit rounds on baking sheet and freeze until solid. Place in large resealable food storage bag and freeze for up to 3 months. Place frozen rounds on a baking sheet and let stand 20 minutes or until thawed. Bake as directed.

Oatmeal Bread

1 cup water
½ teaspoon salt
⅓ cup old-fashioned oats
¼ to ½ cup warm water (105° to 115°F)
1 package (¼ ounce) active dry yeast
3 tablespoons packed light brown sugar or light molasses, divided
2½ cups all-purpose flour
2 tablespoons vegetable oil
Old-fashioned oats (optional)

1. Combine 1 cup water and salt in small saucepan. Bring to a boil. Stir in ⅓ cup oats. Cook over medium heat 5 minutes. Remove from heat and cool until 105° to 115°F.

2. Combine ¼ cup warm water, yeast and 1 tablespoon brown sugar. Stir to dissolve yeast and let stand about 5 minutes or until bubbly.

3. Combine flour, remaining 2 tablespoons brown sugar and oil in food processor; process until well blended, about 15 seconds. Add yeast mixture and oat mixture. Turn on processor and very slowly drizzle just enough remaining water through feed tube so dough forms ball that cleans sides of bowl. Process until ball turns around bowl about 25 times. Turn off processor and let dough stand 1 to 2 minutes.

4. Turn on processor and gradually drizzle in enough remaining water to make dough soft, smooth and satiny but not sticky. Process until dough turns around bowl about 15 times.

5. Turn dough onto lightly floured surface. Shape into ball and place in lightly greased bowl, turning to grease all sides. Cover loosely with plastic wrap; let stand in warm place (85°F) about 1 hour or until doubled in bulk.

6. Punch down dough. Shape into loaf and place in greased 9×5-inch loaf pan. Cover loosely with plastic wrap; let stand in warm place about 45 minutes or until almost doubled in bulk. Sprinkle with additional oats, if desired.

7. Heat oven to 375°F. Bake until golden and loaf sounds hollow when tapped, 25 to 30 minutes. Remove from pan to wire rack; cool.

Makes 1 loaf

Broccoli Cheddar Salad

1 bag (16 ounces) broccoli florets
¼ cup diced red onion
1 tablespoon cider vinegar
½ cup mayonnaise
¼ cup (1 ounce) shredded Cheddar cheese
2 tablespoons raisins
2 tablespoons bacon bits
2 tablespoons sunflower seeds
¼ teaspoon black pepper

1. Bring water to a boil in medium saucepan. Add broccoli; cook 1 minute. Remove to bowl filled with ice water; drain well.

2. Place onion in small bowl. Sprinkle with vinegar. Let sit 1 to 2 minutes to mellow onion flavor.

3. Add broccoli, mayonnaise, cheese, raisins, bacon bits, sunflower seeds and pepper; toss gently to combine.

Makes 6 servings

Corn Pudding

1 tablespoon butter
1 small onion, chopped
1 tablespoon all-purpose flour
2 cups half-and-half
1 cup milk
¼ cup quick-cooking grits or polenta
2 cups corn
4 eggs, lightly beaten
1 can (4 ounces) diced mild chiles, drained
¾ teaspoon salt
¼ teaspoon black pepper
¼ teaspoon hot pepper sauce

1. Preheat oven to 325°F. Grease 11×7-inch baking dish.

2. Melt butter in large saucepan over medium heat. Add onion; cook and stir 5 minutes or until tender and light golden. Stir in flour; cook until golden. Stir in half-and-half and milk; bring to a boil. Whisk in grits; reduce heat to medium-low. Cook and stir 10 minutes or until mixture is thickened.

3. Remove from heat. Stir in corn, eggs, chiles, salt, black pepper and hot pepper sauce. Pour into prepared baking dish. Bake 1 hour or until knife inserted into center comes out clean.   *Makes 8 servings*

Potluck Tip: If prepared in advance, cover and refrigerate up to one day. To serve, microwave at your host's home until heated through. Or wrap baked dish in several layers of aluminum foil and overwrap with thick towel or newspapers to keep finished dish warm when transporting.

Creamed Spinach

3 cups water
2 bags (10 ounces each) fresh spinach, stemmed and
   chopped
2 teaspoons butter
2 tablespoons all-purpose flour
1 cup milk
2 tablespoons grated Parmesan cheese
⅛ teaspoon white pepper
   Ground nutmeg

1. Bring water to a boil; add spinach. Reduce heat; simmer, covered, about 5 minutes or until spinach is wilted. Drain well; set aside.

2. Melt butter in small saucepan over medium-low heat. Stir in flour; cook 1 minute. Whisk in milk; bring to a boil. Whisk constantly 1 to 2 minutes or until mixture thickens. Stir in cheese and pepper.

3. Stir spinach into sauce; heat through. Spoon into serving bowl; sprinkle lightly with nutmeg. Garnish as desired.

Makes 4 servings

This recipe can also be made by substituting 10 ounces frozen chopped spinach. Allow spinach to thaw completely and squeeze out extra liquid before proceeding to step 2.

Savory Summertime Oat Bread

2 teaspoons vegetable oil
½ cup finely chopped onion
4¼ to 4½ cups all-purpose flour, divided
2 cups whole wheat flour
2 cups old-fashioned oats
¼ cup sugar
2 packages (¼ ounce each) rapid-rise active dry yeast
1½ teaspoons salt
1½ cups water
1¼ cups milk
¼ cup butter
1 cup finely shredded carrots
3 tablespoons dried parsley
1 tablespoon butter, melted

1. Heat oil in small nonstick skillet over medium heat. Add onion; cook and stir 3 minutes or until tender.

2. Stir together 1 cup all-purpose flour, whole wheat flour, oats, sugar, yeast and salt in large bowl. Heat water, milk and ¼ cup butter in medium saucepan over low heat until mixture reaches 120° to 130°F. Add to flour mixture; beat with electric mixer at low speed just until moistened. Beat 3 minutes at medium speed. Stir in carrots, onion, parsley and remaining 3¼ to 3½ cups all-purpose flour until dough is no longer sticky.

3. Turn dough out onto lightly floured surface. Knead 5 to 8 minutes or until smooth and elastic. Place in large bowl lightly sprayed with cooking spray, turning to grease all sides. Cover and let rise in warm place (85°F) about 30 minutes or until doubled in bulk. Punch dough down. Cover and let rest 10 minutes.

4. Grease two 8×4-inch loaf pans. Shape dough into two loaves; place in pans. Brush with melted butter. Cover and let rise in warm place 30 minutes or until doubled in bulk.

5. Preheat oven to 350°F. Bake 40 to 45 minutes or until bread sounds hollow when tapped. Remove to wire racks; cool.

Makes 24 servings

Sweet and Sour Red Cabbage

1 slice bacon, chopped
½ cup chopped sweet or yellow onion
4 cups thinly sliced red cabbage (about 9 ounces)
1 red apple, cut into ½-inch chunks
¼ cup cider vinegar
¼ cup honey
½ teaspoon celery salt

1. Cook and stir bacon in large deep skillet over medium heat until crisp. Remove with slotted spoon to transfer bacon to paper towel; set side.

2. Add onion to skillet; cook and stir 5 minutes or until softened. Add cabbage, apple, vinegar, honey and celery salt; mix well. Cook and stir 12 to 14 minutes or until cabbage is crisp-tender and liquid is reduced to glaze.* *Makes 4 servings*

For more tender cabbage, cover and cook 15 minutes. Uncover; cook until liquid is reduced to a glaze.

47

Delicious Desserts

Banana Cream Pie

1 unbaked (9-inch) pie crust
3 medium bananas, divided
1 teaspoon lemon juice
½ cup sugar
6 tablespoons cornstarch
¼ teaspoon salt
3 cups milk
2 egg yolks
1½ teaspoons vanilla
Whipped cream
Cinnamon or powdered sugar (optional)

1. Bake pie crust according to package directions; let cool. Slice 2 bananas; toss with lemon juice. Layer in bottom of pie crust.

2. Combine sugar, cornstarch and salt in medium saucepan. Combine milk and egg yolks in small bowl; slowly stir into sugar mixture. Cook and stir over medium heat until mixture thickens and boils. Boil 1 minute, stirring constantly. Remove from heat; stir in vanilla. Pour into pie shell. Immediately cover with waxed paper. Cool on wire rack. Just before serving, slice remaining banana. Garnish pie with banana, whipped cream and cinnamon or powdered sugar, if desired.

Makes 8 servings

Glazed Applesauce Spice Cake

1 cup packed light brown sugar
¾ cup (1½ sticks) butter, softened
3 eggs
1½ teaspoons vanilla
2¼ cups all-purpose flour
2 teaspoons baking soda
2 teaspoons ground cinnamon
¾ teaspoon ground nutmeg
½ teaspoon ground ginger
¼ teaspoon salt
1½ cups unsweetened applesauce
½ cup milk
⅔ cup chopped walnuts
⅔ cup butterscotch chips
Apple Glaze (recipe follows)

1. Preheat oven to 350°F. Grease and lightly flour 12-cup bundt pan.

2. Beat brown sugar and butter in large bowl with electric mixer at medium speed until light and fluffy. Beat in eggs and vanilla until well blended. Combine flour, baking soda, cinnamon, nutmeg, ginger and salt in medium bowl. Add flour mixture to butter mixture alternately with applesauce and milk, beating well after each addition. Stir in walnuts and butterscotch chips. Spread in prepared pan.

3. Bake 45 to 50 minutes or until toothpick inserted near center comes out clean. Cool in pan 15 minutes. Remove from pan to wire rack; cool completely.

4. Prepare Apple Glaze and spoon over top of cake. Store tightly covered at room temperature. *Makes 10 to 12 servings*

Apple Glaze: Place 1 cup sifted powdered sugar in small bowl. Stir in 2 to 3 tablespoons apple juice concentrate to make stiff glaze.

Strawberry Rhubarb Pie

Pie Dough for a 2-Crust Pie (recipe follows)
4 cups sliced (1-inch pieces) fresh rhubarb
3 cups sliced fresh strawberries
1½ cups sugar
½ cup cornstarch
2 tablespoons quick-cooking tapioca
1 tablespoon grated lemon peel
¼ teaspoon ground allspice
1 egg, lightly beaten

1. Preheat oven to 425°F. Roll out half of pie dough; place in 9-inch pie plate. Trim dough; flute edges, sealing to edge of pie plate. Set aside.

2. Place rhubarb and strawberries in large bowl. Combine sugar, cornstarch, tapioca, lemon peel and allspice in medium bowl; mix well. Sprinkle sugar mixture over fruit; toss to coat well. Fill pie shell with fruit. *Do not mound in center.*

3. Roll out remaining dough to 10-inch circle. Cut into ½-inch-wide strips. Arrange in lattice design over fruit. Brush with egg.

4. Bake 50 minutes or until filling is thick and bubbly. Cool on wire rack. Serve warm or at room temperature.   *Makes 8 servings*

Pie Dough for a 2-Crust Pie: Cut 1 cup (2 sticks) cold butter into small pieces. Combine 2½ cups flour, 1 teaspoon salt and 1 teaspoon sugar in large bowl. Cut in butter with pastry blender or two knives until mixture resembles coarse crumbs. Add 2 tablespoons cold water; stir to blend. Add additional cold water, 1 tablespoon at a time, until dough forms. Knead dough just until it comes together. Divide dough in half. Shape each half into disc; wrap in plastic wrap. Refrigerate at least 1 hour or up to 2 days.

Sugar & Spice Cheesecake

1⅔ cups gingersnap cookie crumbs
⅓ cup butter or margarine, melted
4 packages (8 ounces each) cream cheese, softened
1¼ cups packed brown sugar
3 eggs
1 teaspoon ground cinnamon
1 teaspoon ground nutmeg
½ teaspoon ground cloves
⅓ cup butterscotch chips
1 teaspoon shortening

1. Preheat oven to 375°F. Combine cookie crumbs and butter in small bowl; mix well. Press evenly onto bottom and 1 inch up side of 9-inch springform pan; set aside.

2. Beat cream cheese in large bowl until fluffy; beat in brown sugar. Add eggs, one at a time, beating well after each addition. Blend in cinnamon, nutmeg and cloves.

3. Pour batter into prepared crust. Place springform pan on shallow baking sheet. Bake 45 to 55 minutes or until knife inserted into center comes out clean. Cool to room temperature in pan on wire rack. Cover and refrigerate overnight.

4. Melt butterscotch chips and shortening in small saucepan over low heat, stirring frequently. Drizzle over top of cheesecake. Refrigerate until ready to serve. *Makes 10 to 12 servings*

Old-Fashioned Devil's Food Cake

1½ cups sugar
6 tablespoons butter, softened
3 eggs
1½ teaspoons vanilla
2 cups cake flour
½ cup unsweetened cocoa powder
2 teaspoons baking powder
½ teaspoon salt
½ teaspoon baking soda
1 cup buttermilk
Creamy Chocolate Frosting (page 53)

1. Preheat oven to 350°F. Grease and flour three 8-inch round cake pans.

2. Beat sugar and butter in large bowl with electric mixer at medium speed until fluffy. Beat in eggs and vanilla.

3. Combine flour, cocoa, baking powder, salt and baking soda in medium bowl. Add to butter mixture alternately with buttermilk, beating well after each addition.

4. Spread batter evenly in prepared pans. Bake 25 to 30 minutes or until toothpick inserted into centers comes out clean. Cool in pans on wire racks 10 minutes. Remove from pans to wire racks; cool completely.

5. Meanwhile, prepare Creamy Chocolate Frosting.

6. Place one cake layer on serving plate; spread with frosting. Repeat with remaining two cake layers and frosting. Frost side and top of cake. *Makes 16 servings*

Creamy Chocolate Frosting

5 cups powdered sugar
⅓ cup unsweetened cocoa powder
4 to 6 tablespoons milk, divided
2 tablespoons butter, softened
1 teaspoon vanilla

Beat powdered sugar, cocoa, 4 tablespoons milk, butter and vanilla in large bowl with electric mixer at low speed until smooth, scraping bowl frequently. Beat in additional milk, 1 tablespoon at a time, until desired consistency is reached. *Makes about 2½ cups frosting*

Chilly Lemon Pie

1¼ cups graham cracker crumbs
¼ cup (½ stick) butter, melted
1 tablespoon sugar
1 tablespoon plus 1 teaspoon grated lemon peel, divided
1 can (14 ounces) sweetened condensed milk
½ cup lemon juice (about 3 lemons)
Fresh mint leaves and whipped cream (optional)

1. Preheat oven to 350°F. Combine graham cracker crumbs, butter, sugar and 1 teaspoon lemon peel in 9-inch pie plate until well blended. Press mixture on bottom and up side of pie plate. Bake 7 to 10 minutes or until crust is golden brown. Cool completely.

2. Whisk condensed milk, lemon juice and remaining 1 tablespoon lemon peel in medium bowl until well blended. Pour into prepared crust; cover.

3. Chill 3 hours or until set. Garnish with mint and whipped cream. Refrigerate any leftovers. *Makes 8 servings*

Festive Mincemeat Tartlets

Pie Dough for a 2-Crust Pie (page 50)
1½ cups prepared mincemeat
½ cup chopped peeled and cored tart apple
⅓ cup golden raisins
⅓ cup chopped walnuts
3 tablespoons brandy or frozen apple juice concentrate, thawed
1 tablespoon grated lemon peel

1. Preheat oven to 400°F. Divide pastry in half. Refrigerate one half. Roll remaining half on lightly floured surface to form 13-inch circle. Cut out six 4-inch rounds using cookie cutter. Fit each pastry round into standard (2½-inch) muffin cup. Prick insides of pastries with fork; set aside. Repeat with remaining dough.

2. Bake unfilled pastries 8 minutes. Combine mincemeat, apple, raisins, walnuts, brandy and lemon peel in medium bowl until well blended. Remove crusts from oven; fill each with rounded tablespoonful mincemeat mixture. Press lightly into crust with back of spoon.

3. Bake 18 to 20 minutes more or until edges are golden brown. Cool in pan 5 minutes. Carefully remove from pan to wire rack. Serve warm or cool completely. *Makes 12 tartlets*

Peachy Pecan Cake

1 cup packed brown sugar
1 (8-ounce) package cream cheese, softened
4 eggs, beaten
½ cup half-and-half
1½ teaspoons vanilla
1 cup gingersnap crumbs
1 (6-ounce) package almond brickle chips
¾ cup chopped pecans, toasted*
½ cup coconut flakes
1 (16-ounce) can sliced peaches in juice, drained and
   chopped
Whipped cream (optional)

To toast pecans, spread in single layer on baking sheet. Bake in preheated 350°F oven 8 to 10 minutes or until lightly toasted, stirring occasionally.

1. Preheat oven to 350°F. Grease 9-inch square baking pan.

2. Beat brown sugar and cream cheese in large bowl until well blended.

3. Add eggs, one at a time, beating well after each addition. Blend in half-and-half and vanilla. Stir in gingersnap crumbs, brickle chips, pecans and coconut. Stir in peaches; pour into prepared pan.

4. Bake 35 to 40 minutes or until center is firm and edges are golden brown. Serve warm or chilled. Garnish with whipped cream, if desired. *Makes 9 servings*

Lemon Iced Ambrosia Bars

1¾ cups all-purpose flour, divided
⅓ cup powdered sugar
¾ cup (1½ sticks) cold butter, cut in small pieces
2 cups packed light brown sugar
1 cup flaked coconut
1 cup finely chopped pecans
4 eggs, beaten
½ teaspoon baking powder
   Lemon Icing (recipe follows)

1. Preheat oven to 350°F. Lightly grease 13×9-inch baking pan.

2. Combine 1½ cups flour and powdered sugar in medium bowl; cut in butter with pastry blender or two knives until crumbly. Press onto bottom of prepared pan; bake 15 minutes.

3. Meanwhile, combine remaining ¼ cup flour, brown sugar, coconut, pecans, eggs and baking powder in medium bowl; mix well. Spread evenly over baked crust. Bake 20 to 25 minutes. Cool in pan on wire rack.

4. Prepare Lemon Icing; spread over crust. Cover and refrigerate until set. Cut into bars. Store, covered, in refrigerator.

Makes about 30 bars

Lemon Icing: Stir together 2 cups powdered sugar, 3 tablespoons lemon juice and 2 tablespoons softened butter until smooth. Makes about ⅔ cup.

Brownies

½ **cup unsweetened cocoa powder**
½ **cup boiling water**
1¼ **cups all-purpose flour**
¾ **cup granulated sugar**
¾ **cup packed light brown sugar**
4 **egg whites, lightly beaten**
⅓ **cup vegetable oil**
1½ **teaspoons vanilla**
1 **teaspoon baking powder**
¼ **teaspoon salt**
½ **cup chopped unsalted mixed nuts (optional)**

1. Preheat oven to 350°F. Grease 13×9-inch baking pan.

2. Whisk cocoa and water in large bowl. Stir in flour, granulated sugar, brown sugar, egg whites, oil, vanilla, baking powder and salt; mix well. Fold in chopped nuts, if desired.

3. Pour mixture into prepared pan. Bake 25 minutes or until brownies spring back when lightly touched. *Do not overbake.* Cool in pan on wire rack.

Makes 32 brownies

* * * * * * * * * * * * * * * * *

Spicy Gingerbread Cookies

Cookies
    ¾ cup (1½ sticks) butter, softened
    ⅔ cup light molasses
    ½ cup packed brown sugar
    1 egg
   1½ teaspoons grated lemon peel
   2½ cups all-purpose flour
   1¼ teaspoons ground cinnamon
    1 teaspoon ground allspice
    1 teaspoon vanilla
    ½ teaspoon *each* salt, baking soda and ground ginger
    ¼ teaspoon baking powder

Frosting
    4 cups powdered sugar
    ½ cup (1 stick) butter, softened
    ¼ cup milk
    2 teaspoons vanilla

1. For cookies, beat butter, molasses, brown sugar, egg and lemon peel in large bowl with electric mixer at medium speed until smooth and creamy. Add all remaining cookie ingredients. Reduce speed to low; beat well. Wrap in plastic wrap; refrigerate at least 2 hours.

2. Preheat oven to 350°F. Roll out dough, one half at a time, on well floured surface to ¼-inch thickness. (Keep remaining dough refrigerated.) Cut with 3- to 4-inch cookie cutters. Place on greased cookie sheets. Bake 6 to 8 minutes or until firm. Remove to wire racks; cool completely.

3. For frosting, beat powdered sugar, butter, milk and vanilla in small bowl with electric mixer at low speed until fluffy. Decorate cookies with frosting. *Makes about 4 dozen cookies*

* * * * * * * * * * * * * * * * *

Golden Chiffon Cake

5 eggs, separated
¼ teaspoon cream of tartar
2¼ cups all-purpose flour
1⅓ cups sugar
1 tablespoon baking powder
1 teaspoon salt
¾ cup water
½ cup vegetable oil
1 teaspoon vanilla
½ teaspoon orange extract
Fresh fruit and whipped cream (optional)

1. Preheat oven to 325°F.

2. Beat egg whites and cream of tartar in large bowl until stiff peaks form; set aside. Sift flour, sugar, baking powder and salt into large bowl. Make well in center. Add egg yolks, water, oil, vanilla and orange extract; mix well. Fold in egg white mixture.

3. Immediately spread in ungreased 10-inch tube pan. Bake 55 minutes. *Increase oven temperature to 350°F.* Bake 10 minutes or until cakes springs back when lightly touched with finger. Invert pan onto wire rack; allow cake to cool completely before removing from pan. Garnish with fresh fruit and whipped cream.

Makes 10 to 12 servings

Chiffon cake, created in the 1940s, is characterized by it's use of oil rather than butter or shortening. It gets its spongy texture from whipped egg whites and baking powder.

Fruit and Oat Squares

1 cup all-purpose flour
1 cup quick oats
¾ cup packed light brown sugar
½ teaspoon baking soda
¼ teaspoon salt
¼ teaspoon ground cinnamon
⅓ cup butter or margarine, melted
¾ cup apricot, cherry or other fruit flavor preserves

1. Preheat oven to 350°F. Spray 9-inch square baking pan with nonstick cooking spray; set aside.

2. Combine flour, oats, brown sugar, baking soda, salt and cinnamon in medium bowl; mix well. Add butter; stir with fork until mixture is crumbly. Reserve ¾ cup crumb mixture for topping. Press remaining crumb mixture evenly onto bottom of prepared pan. Bake 5 to 7 minutes or until lightly browned. Spread preserves over crust; sprinkle with reserved crumb mixture.

3. Bake 20 to 25 minutes or until golden brown. Cool completely in pan on wire rack. Cut into 16 squares. *Makes 16 servings*

Hint: Store individually wrapped squares at room temperature up to 3 days or freeze up to 1 month.

Easy Gingerbread

1 sheet (24×12 inches) heavy-duty foil
1 cup all-purpose flour
⅓ cup packed light brown sugar
1 teaspoon ground ginger
¾ teaspoon ground cinnamon
½ teaspoon baking soda
½ teaspoon baking powder
¼ teaspoon salt
¼ teaspoon ground cloves
1 egg
½ cup milk
⅓ cup melted butter
¼ cup unsulphured molasses

1. Preheat oven to 350°F. Gently ease foil into 8×5-inch loaf pan, leaving 1-inch overhang on each side and a 5-inch overhang on both ends. Grease foil.

2. Combine flour, brown sugar, ginger, cinnamon, baking soda, baking powder, salt and cloves in medium bowl; mix well.

3. Beat egg in another medium bowl. Stir in milk, butter and molasses until well mixed.

4. Add liquid mixture to dry ingredients; stir until smooth. Pour batter into prepared pan. Fold overhanging foil sides and ends over batter to cover batter completely; crimp foil, leaving head space for cake as it rises.

5. Bake 45 minutes or until toothpick inserted into center comes out clean. Carefully open foil to allow steam to escape. Cool in pan on wire rack 10 to 15 minutes. Remove gingerbread using foil; remove and discard foil before slicing.   *Makes 6 servings*

Date-Nut Cookies

1 cup chopped dates
½ cup water
1¾ cups all-purpose flour
½ teaspoon baking powder
⅛ teaspoon salt
½ cup packed dark brown sugar
½ cup (1 stick) butter, softened
1 egg
2 teaspoons rum extract
½ cup walnut pieces, chopped

1. Soak dates in water in small bowl at least 30 minutes or up to 2 hours.

2. Preheat oven to 350°F. Grease cookie sheets. Combine flour, baking powder and salt in medium bowl.

3. Beat brown sugar and butter in large bowl with electric mixer at medium speed until smooth. Increase speed to high; beat until light and fluffy. Beat in egg and rum extract until fluffy. Gradually stir in flour mixture alternately with date mixture, mixing just until combined after each addition. Stir in walnuts until blended.

4. Drop level tablespoonfuls of dough about 1½ inches apart onto prepared cookie sheets. Bake 14 minutes or until just set. Remove to wire racks to cool completely. Store in airtight container.

Makes 2 dozen cookies

Index

Metric Conversion Chart

VOLUME MEASUREMENTS (dry)

$^1/_8$ teaspoon = 0.5 mL
$^1/_4$ teaspoon = 1 mL
$^1/_2$ teaspoon = 2 mL
$^3/_4$ teaspoon = 4 mL
1 teaspoon = 5 mL
1 tablespoon = 15 mL
2 tablespoons = 30 mL
$^1/_4$ cup = 60 mL
$^1/_3$ cup = 75 mL
$^1/_2$ cup = 125 mL
$^2/_3$ cup = 150 mL
$^3/_4$ cup = 175 mL
1 cup = 250 mL
2 cups = 1 pint = 500 mL
3 cups = 750 mL
4 cups = 1 quart = 1 L

VOLUME MEASUREMENTS (fluid)

1 fluid ounce (2 tablespoons) = 30 mL
4 fluid ounces ($^1/_2$ cup) = 125 mL
8 fluid ounces (1 cup) = 250 mL
12 fluid ounces (1$^1/_2$ cups) = 375 mL
16 fluid ounces (2 cups) = 500 mL

WEIGHTS (mass)

$^1/_2$ ounce = 15 g
1 ounce = 30 g
3 ounces = 90 g
4 ounces = 120 g
8 ounces = 225 g
10 ounces = 285 g
12 ounces = 360 g
16 ounces = 1 pound = 450 g

DIMENSIONS

$^1/_{16}$ inch = 2 mm
$^1/_8$ inch = 3 mm
$^1/_4$ inch = 6 mm
$^1/_2$ inch = 1.5 cm
$^3/_4$ inch = 2 cm
1 inch = 2.5 cm

OVEN TEMPERATURES

250°F = 120°C
275°F = 140°C
300°F = 150°C
325°F = 160°C
350°F = 180°C
375°F = 190°C
400°F = 200°C
425°F = 220°C
450°F = 230°C

BAKING PAN SIZES

Utensil	Size in Inches/Quarts	Metric Volume	Size in Centimeters
Baking or	8×8×2	2 L	20×20×5
Cake Pan	9×9×2	2.5 L	23×23×5
(square or	12×8×2	3 L	30×20×5
rectangular)	13×9×2	3.5 L	33×23×5
Loaf Pan	8×4×3	1.5 L	20×10×7
	9×5×3	2 L	23×13×7
Round Layer	8×1½	1.2 L	20×4
Cake Pan	9×1½	1.5 L	23×4
Pie Plate	8×1¼	750 mL	20×3
	9×1¼	1 L	23×3
Baking Dish	1 quart	1 L	—
or Casserole	1½ quart	1.5 L	—
	2 quart	2 L	—